Ecology From A to Z

Written & Illustrated by Jacob Angel

Dedication & Acknowledgements

I would like to dedicate this book to my Mom, Gramps, and Grandma Jean. They raised me with unconditional love and support. They have educated me with the knowledge it takes to survive and have always continued to guide me to reach for the stars.

There are several people I would like to acknowledge for their help with Ecology from A to Z. Thanks to my sisters, Roxanne and Claire, for their good nature and support. Thanks to my niece, Jersie Rose, for being such a captive audience to read to, hence inspiring me to write more books to help educate the children of the world. Thanks to Aunt Bernice and Dr. Alice Parker for the key early roles they played in helping me organize my thoughts for this book.

Special thanks to my wife and best friend, Kristi, for pushing me to strive for excellence and always being the recycle police everywhere we go. Thank you, Mom and Kristi, for your patience, love, friendship, and tremendous help getting this book to print.

Much love and thanks to all of the very special dogs that have enriched my life and inspired characters in my books: Indi, Maggie, Jazz, Aspen, Nanook, and Bagheera of Ula Mountain. ☺

~ Ecology From A to Z ~

My name is Bo Bo Darling,
And something strange happened to me.
As I was walking through the forest,
I met Irv, the turtle under a tree.

Irv asked, " Do you know what Ecology is?
You really need to know!
It is everything that protects our planet,
And helps the Earth to grow."

"Some people just don't know,
About the Earth we see.
So come with me and learn about,
Ecology from A to Z."

~ A ~

Atmosphere

Why did the turtle stop me?
At first I had no clue.
Though it was a really pretty day,
And I had nothing else to do.

He said, "I've been watching you closely,
What you've done is just not right.
You are destroying the atmosphere,
Which could be quite a fright."

"Atmosphere is the space around the Earth,
The hot and cold which surrounds us all.
It carries the air we need to breathe,
To grow healthy, strong, and tall."

"I know that by spraying bug repellent,
You're trying to keep the bugs away,
But all of that aerosol spayed into the air,
Will destroy the atmosphere more each day."

TRASH CAN
DRINK BOX

~ B ~

Biodegradable

"I also saw you eat your lunch,
You left your trash on the bench to rot.
If it were biodegradable it would wear away,
But some of it simply was not."

"For instance the juice box that held your drink
Would take a long time to decay,
Whereas the apple core you left on the bench,
Will be gone in a couple of days."

"Please remember not everything is biodegradable,
And we can choose what we buy.
Choosing food and toys with less packaging
Will keep the landfills from reaching the sky."

"Always put trash in it's proper place,
As a dirty world is one of my greatest fears.
If we can't get together and lend a hand,
The world will be dirty for years."

~ C ~

Carbon Monoxide

Irv turned, looked at me, and said,
"Let us take a detour on this walk."
So I went with the turtle down the path,
And he continued with his talk.

"Carbon Monoxide, or CO,
Pollutes the air we breathe.
Some machines, such as cars, produce too much,
And that's not what we need."

Irv pointed his arm to the city,
And said, "Look at all of that smoke.
If people continue such carelessness,
We will all begin to choke."

"By taking the bus or riding your bike,
There will be less CO.
With your parents', friends', and neighbors' help,
The sky will always glow."

~ D ~

Drought

As we continued to travel,
Down the twisted trail,
We came upon a fish named Keith,
Who carried water in a pail.

I asked the fish, "What are you doing?
You're walking out of your river?"
He replied, "My river's run dry,
I must fill it before I quiver!"

By taking shorter showers,
And turning the water off while brushing your teeth,
You can help conserve water,
So there is more for fish like Keith.

~ E ~

Endangered Species

The path led to the ocean,
Where we met Jersie, a great Blue Whale.
She asked us to sit down,
And told us a frightening tale.

"For many, many years,
My cousins have been killed,
By hunters with big fishing spears,
Who are very, very skilled."

"When hunters try to hurt me,
Nowadays they fail,
Because caring people such as you,
Can join clubs to save the whales!"

~ F ~

Farming

Jersie took us for a ride,
She dropped us off at a farm.
Irv told me what the farmer was doing,
Would cause the environment harm.

"Farming can be good for the soil and the land,
But spraying pesticide on the crops is not.
Organic farming is poison free,
And will help out the environment a lot."

"Try to remember when you are planting,
Do it in an organic way.
You will make the world around us all,
Healthier in every way."

GARBAGE
DUMP

~ G ~

Garbage

Irv and I kept on walking,
And noticed a garbage dump.
Irv turned to me and said,
"This makes my shell slump."

"There are so many things in this trash,
That could be used again.
Everything from rubber tires,
To cans that were made from tin."

The paper, plastic, and glass
Also should not be here.
If everyone would recycle their waste,
This dump would get smaller each year.

"If you make organized piles of garbage,
Before it comes time to discard,
Then taking the recyclables out,
Will not seem so hard."

To JUNgle
oil
XXX
oil

~ H ~

Hazardous Waste

"There are lots of items in the garbage,
That can arouse some distaste.
Some of them you have learned about,
Others are called hazardous waste."

"This includes aerosols, pesticides,
Paint cans, and oil.
These can cause permanent damage,
To all of our precious soil."

"Please remember to tell your folks,
To put hazardous waste in it's place.
All things, good or bad,
Have been given a proper space."

~ I ~

Industrial Waste

Irv and I walked into a jungle,
Until we were in the middle.
What do you know, there we saw,
An elephant playing a fiddle.

I asked the elephant what she was doing,
And what was her name.
She said, "Hi, my name is Barbara Sue,
And playing the blues is my game."

I asked her why she seemed so sad,
Was there anything I could do?
She said, "Industrial waste has polluted the river,
And it's gotten me feeling blue."

Industrial Waste is produced by activity,
Of industries both big and small.
From mills to mines to factories,
That make items to fill the mall.

Irv said, "By not polluting the waters,
Healthier animals will be seen.
Barbara Sue will have to take up Jazz,
As her river will be clean!"

~ J ~

Job

Irv glanced around the jungle and said,
"I hope you're beginning to know,
That it is your job to tell everyone,
How to help the world to grow."

"Jobs can be as simple as,
Picking up litter that you see.
Sharing new information with your friends,
Would really be easy!"

"To help conserve energy,
Instead of a vacuum, use a broom.
Always remember to turn off the lights,
When you leave a room."

"No job that you can do is too small,
Or of little weight.
Any job to help ecology,
Will make you feel so great."

Kids
Against
Pollution

~ K ~
Kids Against Pollution

"Now that you know it's your job,
To help the environment grow.
Let's just say that there is something else,
That you need to know."

"There are many clubs you can join or form,
To help preserve ecology.
There are groups such as Kids Against Pollution,
With interesting websites for you to see."

"You too can be a kid against pollution,
There are so many things you can do.
Get a neighborhood group together,
That will help fight pollution with you."

~ L ~

Littering

I found a piece of candy,
A gum drop big and round.
I put it in my mouth,
And threw the wrapper on the ground.

Irv said, "I can't believe what I just saw!
Have you heard anything I've said?
Or has everything I've told you,
Already left your head?"

"Littering is a NO NO!
It's a habit that is bad.
It will clutter up the forest,
And will make me very sad."

~ M ~
Metal

We came upon a clearing,
And found a kangaroo.
I said, "my name is Bo Bo Darling.
Hello, and how do you do?"

She said, "My name is Bernice,
I'm collecting cans in my pouch.
In some states you get money to recycle,
I think I'll buy a new couch."

"Metal does not biodegrade,
It should never be thrown away.
A natural resource used again and again,
That's so important today."

"Silver, gold, aluminum, and copper,
Precious metals mined from the land.
Once they're gone, they're gone,
So try hard to pitch in a hand."

Notes
- Start to Recycle CANS.
- Turn off the WATER when I AM brushing My teeth.
- Do not litter.

~ N ~
Note Taking

I said goodbye to Bernice,
And down the path we did run.
It was at that point I realized,
I was having lots of fun.

I was excited learning from Irv,
He taught me things I did not know.
If I thought that I'd forget,
Note taking was the way to go.

By taking notes on what you learn,
And the proper way to discard.
You'll learn how to save planet Earth,
No job will seem too hard.

~ O ~
Ozone

Irv raced down the trail,
He is really very fast.
"There's a layer around the Earth called the ozone,
And without our help, it won't last."

"We need to spread the word,
About things that we can do,
To slow down the depleting ozone layer,
And keep the sky bright blue."

"Aerosols and pollution,
Are things we can do without.
Without their use the ozone stays thicker,
And we'll smile instead of pout."

~ P ~

Pollution

We walked until we hit a beach,
That seemed to be quite a mess.
With everything from bottles to tires,
Even an old baby doll dress.

Irv said, "Think about the sea life,
Pollution is not just here on this shore.
It becomes their toys when it floats out to sea,
And that leads to them ending up sore."

"For example, a dolphin plays with a plastic cup,
And it gets caught around his nose.
I once saw a giant octopus,
With seven legs stuck in a hose."

"Remember that everything in the world,
Has been given a certain spot.
By putting garbage in it's proper place,
You are fighting pollution a lot."

~ Q ~

Questions

"You may have a lot of questions so far,
And things you want to know.
There are several different places
You can go to for info."

"Info is short for information,
Which is what we all need.
It is the answers to all of your questions,
All you do is read."

"My favorite place to go,
Is the library or the internet.
I make sure that I take notes
So that I will not ever forget."

"There are lots of places,
That you can direct your questions to.
If they're good 'eco' friendly businesses,
They will try hard to help you."

~ R ~

Rainforest

We entered a forest full of rain.
The rain lasted for an hour.
It was not too cold,
And was as refreshing as a shower.

Irv said, "We're in the rainforest,
A place that is really neat.
There is wonderful life in this forest,
That you may be able to meet."

Just then I met a snake,
Who said, "Hello, my name is Sly."
He was speckled purple,
With one blue and one yellow eye.

He said "People hurt the forests,
To graze their cows and hogs.
They cut down the trees,
And turn them into logs."

"By joining clubs to save the rainforest,
There is not much you have to give.
Endangered creatures, such as I,
Will have a place to live."

~ S ~

Sea Water

Irv and I traveled over a bridge,
And looked down upon the sea.
Irv pointed at something in the sea water,
That really bothered me.

I saw a great big tire,
And some plastic floating around.
We met a black goose named Baggy,
Who was making a horrible sound.

He said he was swimming one day,
When he thought he had encountered some soil.
What he found out was,
He had been swimming in dirty oil.

How did the oil get into the sea water?
Baggy said, “I do not know.
Just remember to put trash in its proper place,
And clean sea water will always flow.”

~ T ~

Turtle

On the other side of the bridge,
We sat down on a log.
We saw a bunch of turtles running,
From what sounded like a dog.

Irv explained that what I heard,
Was not a dog at all.
It was a mean turtle hunter,
Practicing his turtle call.

Irv told me as we were hiding,
That the hunter wanted his shell.
Turtles are hunted for their beautiful shells,
And meat to cook and sell.

By refusing to buy items,
Made from the turtle and his threatened friends,
Animals like Irv, Jersie, and Sly,
Will be off the Endangered list again.

~ U ~
Ultraviolet Light

Through the path we walked until,
We came upon a magical place.
It seemed to be very dark,
As if we were in outer space.

I heard a voice say "Welcome to the future,
Let us have some fun."
But all I wanted to know was,
What happened to the sun?

Irv told me if no one takes a step,
To improve the ecology,
The ozone layer will be very thin,
And not filter enough UV.

UV stands for ultraviolet light.
The sun puts it out each day.
If too much filters through the ozone layer,
We will have to stay out of the sun to play.

Veggie Bar

~ V ~
Vegetation

As we came back into present time,
I had a new found love for light.
All of the colors seemed so beautiful,
Especially the garden to my right.

Irv took me to a veggie bar,
Where I could get something to eat.
Everything on the menu was made from the farm,
It was really quite a treat.

"These are healthy organic foods,
You can eat them in many ways.
Or blend them into smoothies,
You'll feel energized for days."

"Vegetation is all of the plant life,
It grows in the cold and the hot.
It puts oxygen into the air,
And helps us breathe a lot."

~ W ~

Wildlife

Irv and I walked back through the rainforest,
And then into a mystical space.
It was a journey through a dream Irv shared,
About wildlife that could've lived in this place.

I met a creature called an Inflingle Hopper,
And it really was quite nice.
It never would harm anything,
From elephants to mice.

The Inflingle Hopper said to me,
"Some wildlife like me, you'll never be able to know,
Because people have changed the forest,
And hurt wildlife they never let grow."

"Wildlife is anything,
From animals, insects, and trees.
The birds and the fish,
The flowers swaying in the breeze."

"It is important to preserve the land we live on,
Take care of the wildlife that's around."
Then he was gone, in a burst of stars...
Only his footprints were left on the ground.

indi

~ X ~

Xeriscaping (farming on dry land)

On the other side of the rainforest,
There's a dog growing a farm.
She said her name is Indi,
As she greeted me with her arm.

She told me that her farm was different,
On a hilltop her land sits high.
It is difficult for her to water the garden.
So she farms on land that is dry.

Irv told me "This is called Xeriscaping,
And it's very easy to do.
It's good for the environment,
And can look very pretty, too."

"Lavender, Thyme, Figs, and Aloe,
Are all great things to grow.
By Xeriscaping these products,
Indi's efforts sure do glow!"

"The aroma of lavender and thyme are great,
And the figs taste like they should.
The aloe's so soothing on my skin,
It feels really good!"

CANS
PAPER
PLAS

~ Y ~
Yard Waste

Irv said "It's getting kind of late,
You need to get home for bed."
I told Irv that I had plans,
To clean up my backyard instead.

"Let me help you get started,
I'll walk with you home.
Hopefully those who help the environment,
Will not be alone."

We walked through my backyard,
And saw a great big mess.
Irv said, " No need to worry,
This is no reason to stress."

"We'll pile up the leaves,
And add food scraps gone bad.
It turns into plant food called mulch,
The backyard will be glad."

BoBo
Darling

~ Z ~
Zoo

As I laid down in my bed,
I saw my turtle pal.
He said, "Get some sleep Bo Bo Darling,
I am going to go meet my gal."

"Tomorrow I would like to go,
To a place that is called the zoo.
There you can see more animals,
And ecological jobs you can do."

"So please remember everything,
You learned with me today.
I look forward to tomorrow,
Where we can meet again and play."

"There are always things to learn,
And lots more to observe.
I'll be your partner anytime,
Just think out loud.....
...................................IRRRRRRRRRRV!!!!!"

In very loving and happy memories of K.D.G.

Keith David Grinstein

Ecology from A to Z
A creation from Angel's Food for Thought,
A division of Angel's Food, Orcas Island, WA

Written and Illustrated by Jacob Angel, 1993
Edited by Jacob and Kristi Angel, 2008

Printed and bound in the USA.

ISBN - 13
978-0-9815824-0-5
ISBN - 10
0-9815824-0-0

Printed on Recycled Paper by Bang Printing.

Angel's Food for Thought and Bang Printing are proud signers of the Treatise for Responsible Paper Use. The treatise, guided by Green Press Initiative, is a declaration of best environmental practices for the book industry. For more information on the treatise, please go to: http://www.greenpressinitiative.org/

Notes

Notes

Notes

Notes